ANIMAL BATTLES

WATER BUFFALO VS. DHOLE PACK

BY NATHAN SOMMER

TORQUE

TORQUE, AN IMPRINT OF BELLWETHER MEDIA BY FLUTTERBEE

Torque brims with excitement perfect for thrill-seekers of all kinds. Discover daring survival skills, explore uncharted worlds, and marvel at mighty engines and extreme sports. In *Torque* books, anything can happen. Are you ready?

This edition first published in 2027 by Bellwether Media, Inc.

For information regarding permission, write to Bellwether Media, Inc., Attention: Permissions Department, 3500 American Blvd W, Suite 150, Bloomington, MN 55431.

Library of Congress Cataloging-in-Publication Data is available at www.loc.gov or upon request from the publisher.

ISBN: 9798898801168 (hardcover)
ISBN: 9798898802752 (paperback)
ISBN: 9798898802400 (ebook)

Editor: Suzane Nyguen Designer: Josh Brink

Printed in the United States of America, North Mankato, MN.

TABLE OF CONTENTS

THE COMPETITORS

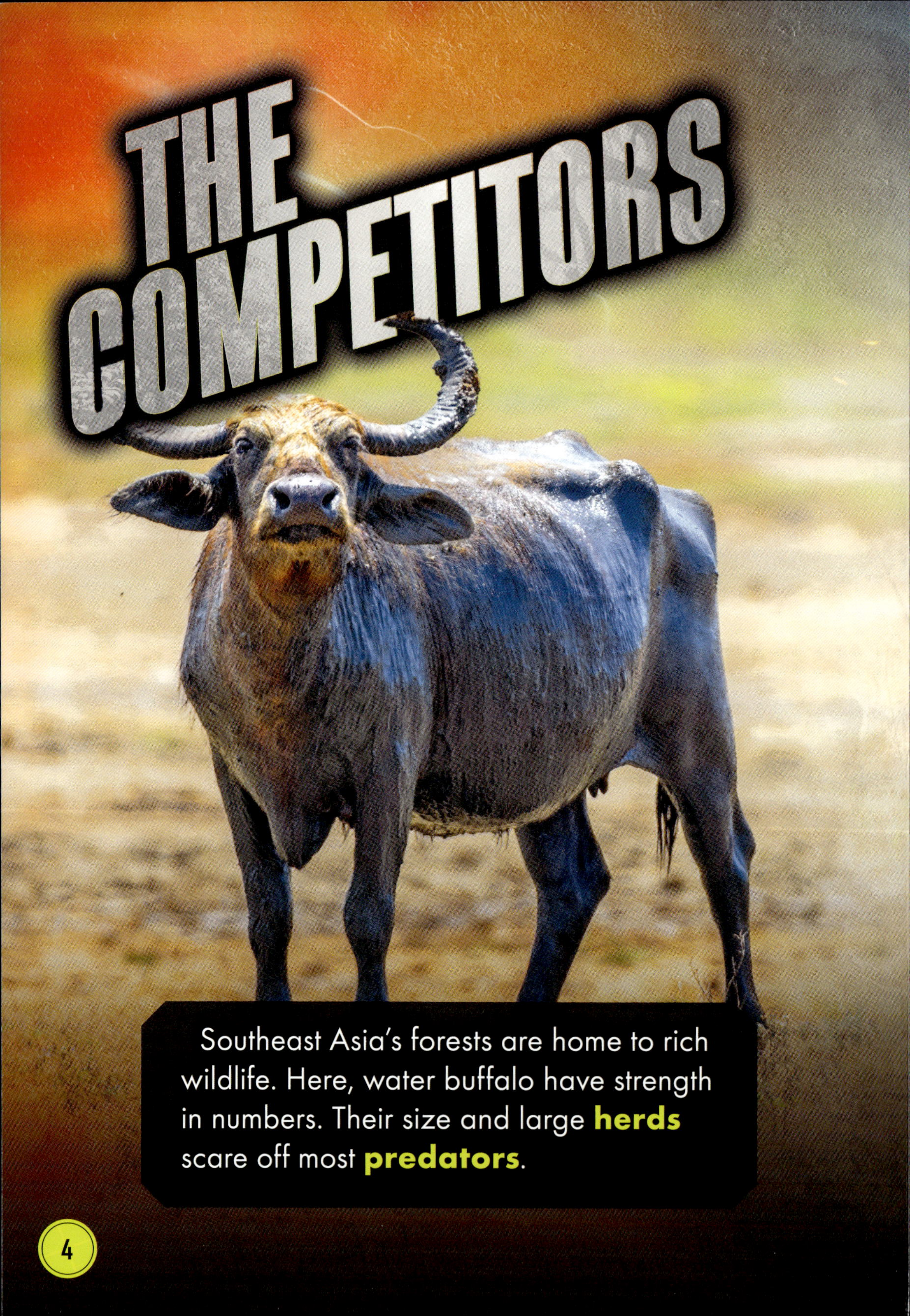

Southeast Asia's forests are home to rich wildlife. Here, water buffalo have strength in numbers. Their size and large **herds** scare off most **predators**.

Water buffalo share some **habitats** with dholes. These wild dogs have the energy to overpower **prey** of all sizes. What happens when these two groups come face-to-face?

Water buffalo are one of the largest **bovines**. They weigh up to 2,645 pounds (1,200 kilograms). They grow up to around 6 feet (1.8 meters) tall at the shoulder. The buffalo can be black or gray. Large, curved horns grow from their narrow heads.

Water buffalo are found in parts of Southeast Asia. They live in **tropical** forests and wet grasslands.

LIVING TRACTORS

Water buffalo are common farm animals. They are nicknamed "living tractors" for their strong pulling power.

WILD WATER BUFFALO PROFILE

HEIGHT

UP TO 6 FEET
(1.8 METERS)

WEIGHT

UP TO 2,645 POUNDS
(1,200 KILOGRAMS)

HABITATS

FORESTS

GRASSLANDS

SWAMPS

WILD WATER BUFFALO RANGE

DHOLE PROFILE

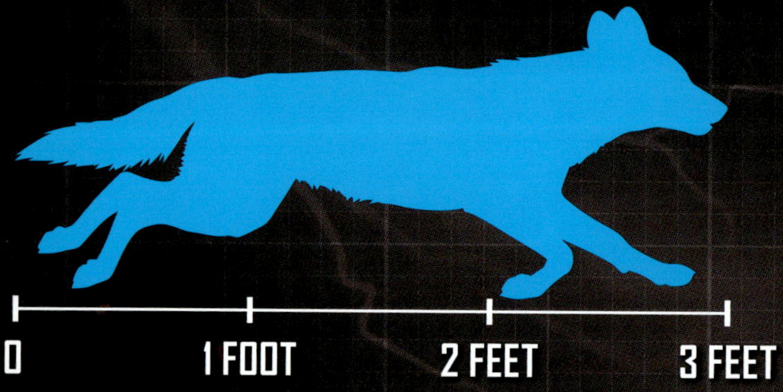

LENGTH (WITH TAIL)

UP TO 3 FEET
(0.9 METERS)

WEIGHT

UP TO 46 POUNDS
(21 KILOGRAMS)

HABITATS

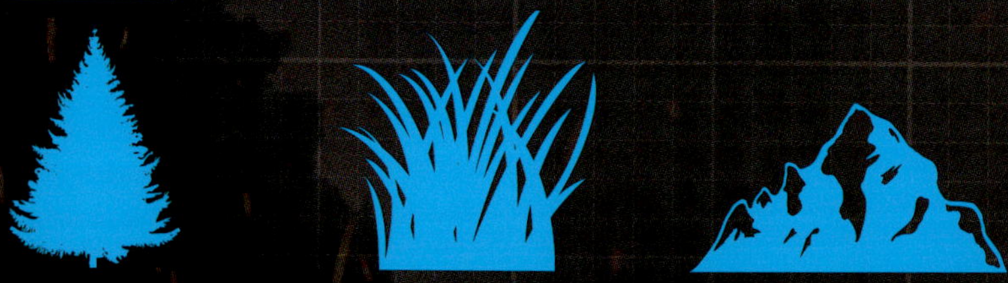

FORESTS

GRASSLANDS

MOUNTAINS

DHOLE RANGE

Dholes are wild dogs. They have reddish-brown coats with white bellies. Their long, **bushy** tails have black tips. Large, rounded ears sit atop their heads.

Dholes are found in eastern and southern Asia. They prefer forests near water and open grasslands. The dogs hunt in packs with up to 30 members.

DIFFERENT DOGS

Dholes have thicker noses and mouths than most dogs. They also have two fewer teeth.

SECRET WEAPONS

Water buffalo live in herds with up to 30 members. They fight together to protect against enemies. The buffalo charge together to defeat predators such as tigers.

Dholes are some of the most social dogs. Packs **communicate** using many different calls. They make high-pitched whistles to stick together while hunting. This helps them **track** and defeat large prey.

Water buffalo have large, wide **hooves**. These help them move easily in mud without sinking or getting stuck. They are also used as weapons to kick enemies.

Strong legs make dholes very **athletic**. They can swim and chase prey for long distances without tiring. The dogs can jump 7 feet (2.1 meters) into the air.

SECRET WEAPONS

WATER BUFFALO

TEAMWORK

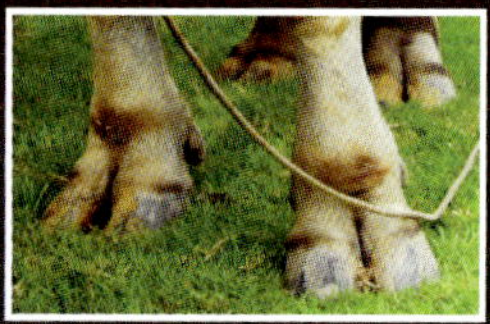
LARGE HOOVES

LONG HORNS

WATER BUFFALO HORNS VS. SOFA LENGTH

WATER BUFFALO HORNS
OVER 6 FEET (1.8 METERS)

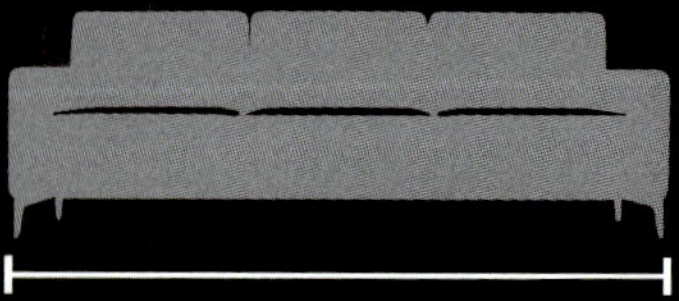

SOFA
7 FEET (2.1 METERS)

Water buffalo horns are over 6 feet (1.8 meters) across. The buffalo stay cool by using these to shovel mud onto themselves. They also ram their horns into enemies.

SECRET WEAPONS

DHOLE

COMMUNICATION

STRONG LEGS

POWERFUL JAWS

Dholes have powerful jaws with sharp teeth. They use these to quickly and easily tear apart prey. Multiple bites from pack members often defeat large animals.

ATTACK MOVES

Water buffalo form lines or circles when they sense danger. Young and weak buffalo stand behind larger buffalo. This formation makes it harder for enemies to attack.

Dhole packs **ambush** their prey. They often chase prey toward water or other pack members. Packs can surround and attack animals up to ten times their body weight.

SURPRISING SPEED

Water buffalo are fast for their size. They can run up to 30 miles (48 kilometers) per hour.

Water buffalo attack predators that come too close. They line up and charge. Herds scatter to **slash** attackers horn-first from different angles.

Dholes defeat large prey with repeated bites to the rear. They strike smaller animals in the head. The dogs often eat prey while it is still alive!

POUNDS OF MEAT

One dhole can eat 8.8 pounds (4 kilograms) of meat per hour.

READY, FIGHT!

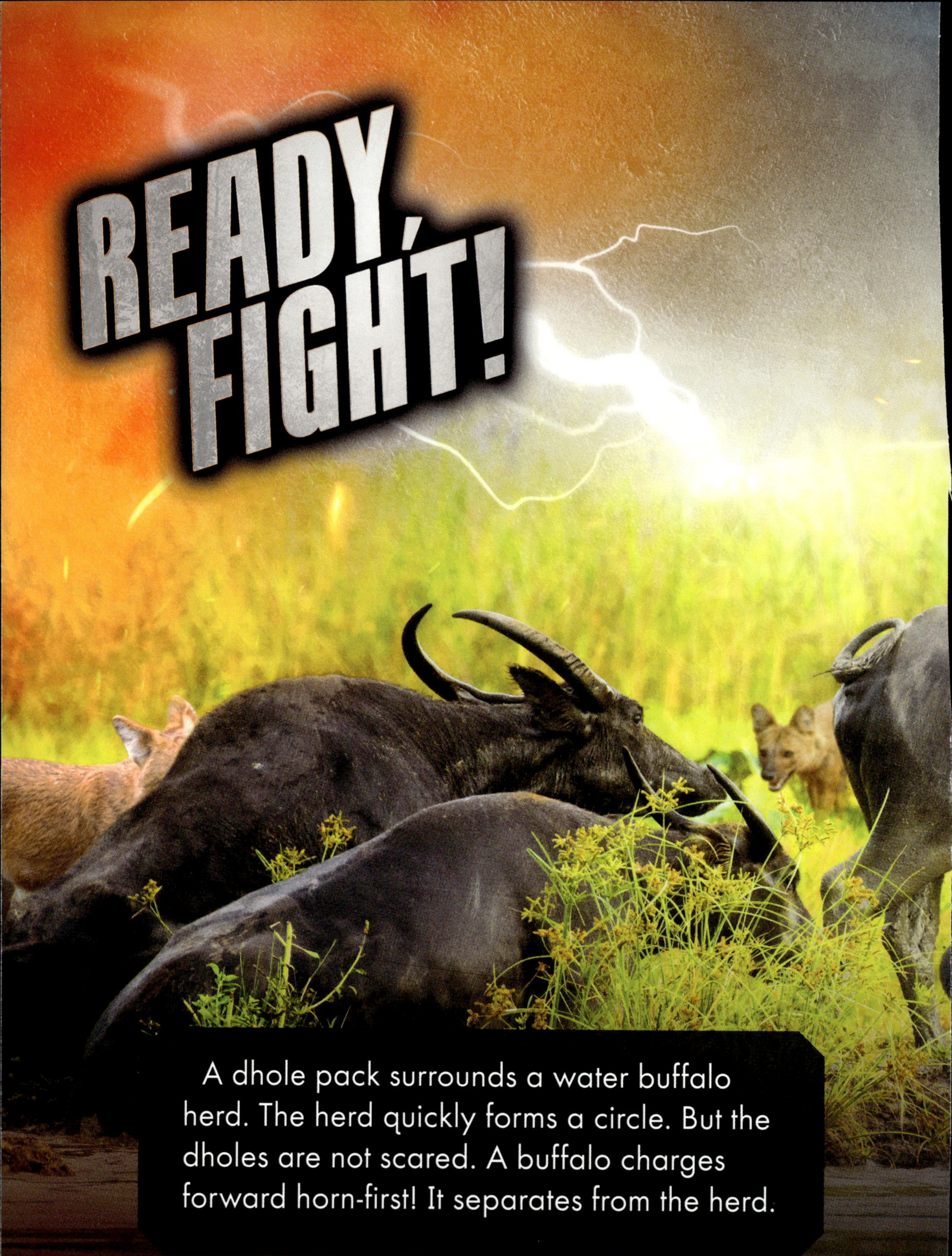

A dhole pack surrounds a water buffalo herd. The herd quickly forms a circle. But the dholes are not scared. A buffalo charges forward horn-first! It separates from the herd.

The dogs chase the separated buffalo. The buffalo kicks at the pack. But the dogs leap on its rear to bite it. Few animals can outlast a hungry dhole pack!

GLOSSARY

ambush—to carry out a surprise attack

athletic—fit and active

bovines—members of the bovine family; the bovine family includes cowlike animals such as bison, oxen, and bulls.

bushy—thick and furry

communicate—to share thoughts and feelings using sounds, faces, and actions

habitats—the homes or areas where animals prefer to live

herds—groups of animals that live and travel together

hooves—hard covers on the feet of some animals

predators—animals that hunt other animals for food

prey—animals that are hunted by other animals for food

slash—to cut with a sharp object

track—to look for prey by following marks left behind, like scents

tropical—having to do with a place that is hot and wet

TO LEARN MORE

AT THE LIBRARY

Daniels, Ruby. *Cape Buffalo.* Minneapolis, Minn.: ABDO, 2025.

Sommer, Nathan. *African Wild Dog Pack vs. Leopard.* Minneapolis, Minn.: Bellwether Media, 2024.

Sommer, Nathan. *Arctic Wolf Pack vs. Polar Bear.* Minneapolis, Minn.: Bellwether Media, 2025.

ON THE WEB

FACTSURFER

Factsurfer.com gives you a safe, fun way to find more information.

1. Go to www.factsurfer.com.
2. Enter "water buffalo vs. dhole pack" into the search box and click 🔍.
3. Select your book cover to see a list of related content

INDEX

The images in this book are reproduced through the courtesy of: serejkakovalev, front cover (water buffalo); Wirestock, front cover (dhole); voravuds, pp. 2 (water buffalo), 3 (water buffalo), 20 (water buffalo), 21 (water buffalo), 22 (water buffalo), 23 (water buffalo), 24 (water buffalo); Rahuldev Rajguru, pp. 2 (dhole 1), 3 (dhole 1), 20 (dhole 1), 21 (dhole 1), 22 (dhole 1), 23 (dhole 1), 24 (dhole 1); Banu R, pp. 2 (dhole 2), 3 (dhole 2), 20 (dhole 2), 21 (dhole 2), 22 (dhole 2), 23 (dhole 2), 24 (dhole 2); Nilanka Sampath, p. 4; NaturesMomentsuk, p. 5; Nabin Clicks, pp. 6-7; Chaithanya Krishnan, pp. 8-9; Endemic India, p. 10; SITTICHOK KLANGWICHEAN, p. 11; Piotr Poznan, p. 12; STORM INSIDE PHOTOGRAPHY, p. 12 (hooves); Shashank Birla/ Alamy Stock Photo, p. 13; TraceRouda, p. 14 (teamwork); Teerawut, p. 14 (large hooves); Sourav_Ganguli, p. 14 (long horns); blickwinkel/ Alamy Stock Photo, p. 14 (water buffalo); belizar, p. 15 (communication); Nick Garbutt/ Garbutt, Nick/ SuperStock, p. 15 (strong legs); Karina Schultze, p. 15 (powerful jaws); Mark Malkinson/ Alamy Stock Photo, p. 15 (dhole); Maithreebhanu, p. 16; chuchart duangdaw/ Getty Images, p. 17; Neverse, p. 18; mkkuppuraj, p. 19.